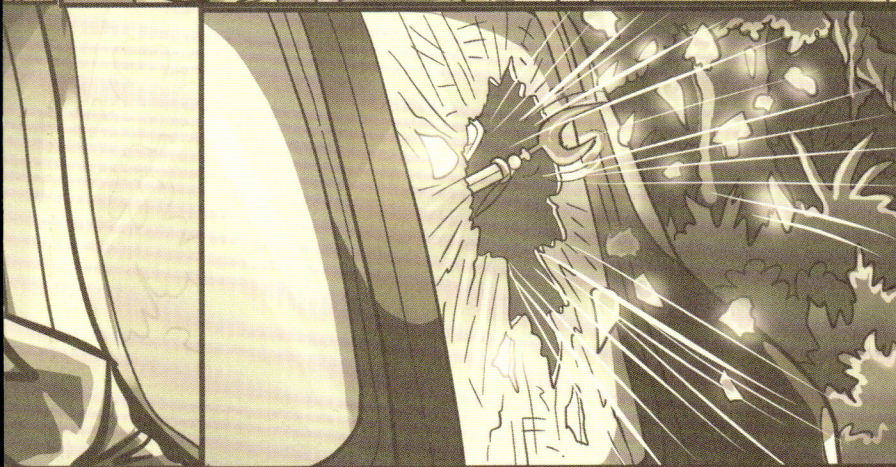

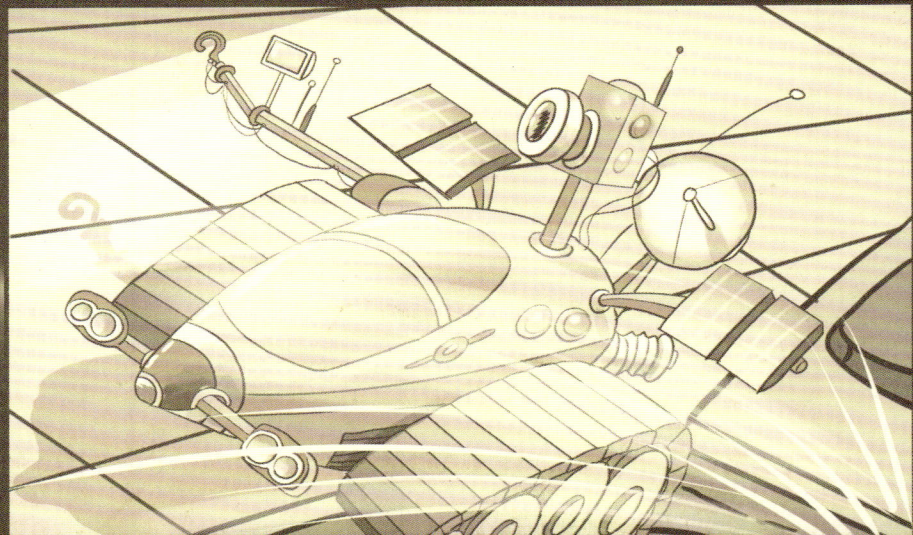

Prepared for print by
The Circle magazine

Translated by
Chaya Sara Ben Shachar

Edited by
Deena Weinberg

Project Manager:
S. Loberbom

Cover Design:
pirsum@duvdvan.co.il

Distributed By:

Lechaim לחיים

Lechaim Productions Inc.
Tel: 718-369-2090, Fax: 718-369-2092
1529 Dean Street, Brooklyn NY 11213
info@lchaimusa.com
www.lchaimusa.com

Eli & Sruly and the Flashes in the Dark

By **Motty Heller** ▪ Written by: Hadas Irenstein

הוועדה הרוחנית לבקורת ספרי קריאה
"עיני לאה"
ע"ש הרבנית לאה אויערבך ע"ה

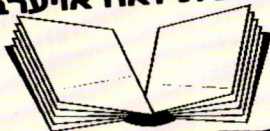

בנשיאות הגאון ר ישראל גנס שליט"א
ירושלים עיה"ק 050-4122756

אישור

הננו לאשר שנציג הוועדה עבר על הספר "צופן מסנוור"
מאת **מוטי הלר** ואישר את הקריאה בו.

"חלק נוסף בסדרת הספרים אלי ושרולי, עוד סיפור עם
עלילה מרתקת וסוף טוב.

והנה באשר האות הכתובה משמשת אמצעי חינוכי רב
השפעה, על כן יש חשיבות לוועדה החשובה הזאת שהיא צורך
השעה בדור אשר כל מושך בקולמוס יכול בנקל - עקב שכלולי
הטכנולוגיה – להו"ל כל אשר יעלה על לבו.

MARCH 17, 1992:
A POWERFUL BOMB EXPLODED NEAR THE ISRAELI EMBASSY IN BUENOS AIRES, ARGENTINA, KILLING 29 PEOPLE.

BOOM!

JULY 18, 1994:
ANOTHER EXPLOSION ROCKED THE JEWISH COMMUNITY OF BUENOS AIRES.

AT 10 A.M., A SUICIDE BOMBER DETONATED A CAR OUTSIDE THE JEWISH COMMUNITY CENTER, KILLING 85 PEOPLE.

THIS WAS CONSIDERED ONE OF THE WORST TERROR ATTACKS IN THE HISTORY OF ARGENTINA.

CLASSIFIED INFORMATION REVEALED THAT A THIRD ATTACK HAD BEEN THWARTED BY THE MOSSAD AND ISRAEL'S GENERAL SECURITY SERVICES.

7

OCTOBER, 2018
WE NEED TO PULL OFF ANOTHER TERRORIST ATTACK SOON, OR ELSE...
OR ELSE, WHAT?
YOU DON'T REALLY EXPECT AN ANSWER TO THAT QUESTION, DO YOU?
OF COURSE NOT. IF WE DON'T PLAN AN ATTACK SOON, THEY'LL STOP FUNDING US, RIGHT?
WORSE!
OH, NO. WE'D BETTER COME UP WITH A PLAN.
FIRST WE NEED A TARGET.
WE HAVE A TARGET ALREADY. INSTEAD OF ARGENTINA, WE'RE MOVING ON TO SOUTH AFRICA.
WE'RE GOING TO HAVE TO HIRE SOMEONE NEW FOR THIS MISSION.
YES! WE'RE ON TO BIG THINGS NOW.

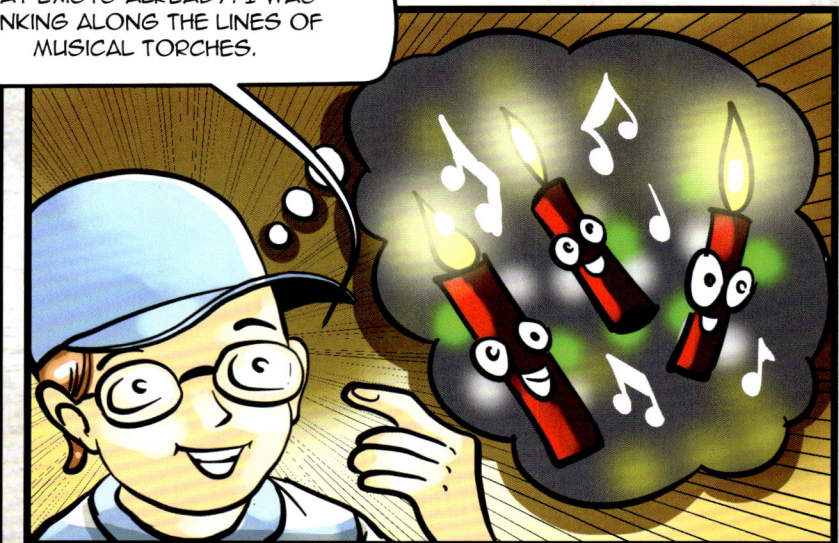

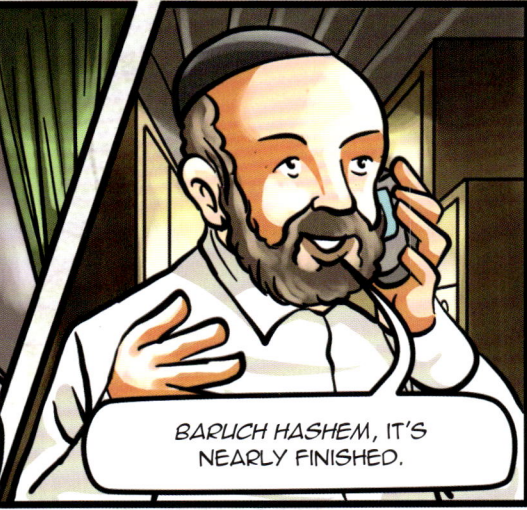

ROBI, YOU NEED TO STAY IN THERE WITHOUT ANY TALKING, BLINKING, OR BEEPING. IS THAT CLEAR?

QUIET ROBI. ROBI IS QUIET.

ZZZZIP.

LOOK AT THAT MAN, SRULI. DO YOU THINK THE PLANE WILL HAVE ENOUGH ROOM FOR ALL OF HIS LUGGAGE?

DIDN'T YOU TELL ABBA THAT WE WOULDN'T LOOK FOR ADVENTURES ON THIS TRIP?

YOU'RE RIGHT.

AS USUAL.

HEY, THAT MAN LEFT SOMETHING ON THE BENCH.

IN THE SOUTH AFRICAN HEADQUARTERS:
THAT'S THE PLACE.
THIS IS THE TIME.
12:00
AND THESE ARE WHAT THE RESULTS SHOULD BE.
WE'LL CATCH THOSE JEWS COMPLETELY BY SURPRISE. THEY HAVE NO IDEA WHAT THEY'RE IN FOR.
WE HAVE 200 POUNDS OF EXPLOSIVES IMPATIENTLY AWAITING DETONATION.
TIME TO TELL THE BIG BOSS THAT WE'RE READY, RIGHT?
ABSOLUTELY. ZERO HOUR'S ALMOST HERE!
RABBI ZEVULON? OF COURSE, I'D BE HAPPY TO COME WITH YOU TO THE AIRPORT TO GREET THE SCRIBE AND HIS FAMILY.

ON THE PLANE:
MAYBE WE SHOULD USE THE FLASHLIGHTS TO CREATE A TYPE OF MORSE CODE.
WHAT'S MORSE CODE?
MORSE CODE IS A FAMOUS CODE THAT USES DOTS AND DASHES. IF I SHINE THE FLASHLIGHT FOR A SECOND, THAT WOULD BE ONE DOT, AND IF I SHINE IT FOR LONGER THAT WOULD BE A LINE. IF I TURN IT OFF, THAT WOULD BE LIKE A SPACE. DOES THAT MAKE SENSE?
ER... IT SOUNDS COMPLICATED, ACTUALLY.
HEY, SRULI! LOOK, THE FLASHLIGHT HAS LETTERS ON IT. IT'S LIKE A BUILT-IN CODE!
ROBI, GIVE THE FLASHLIGHT BACK RIGHT NOW! AND GET BACK INTO THE SUITCASE IMMEDIATELY!
LOOK, IF I PRESS A LETTER ON THE FLASHLIGHT, IT SHINES THAT LETTER IN THE AIR.
ACB
SOPHISTICATED SIGNALING FLASHLIGHT!

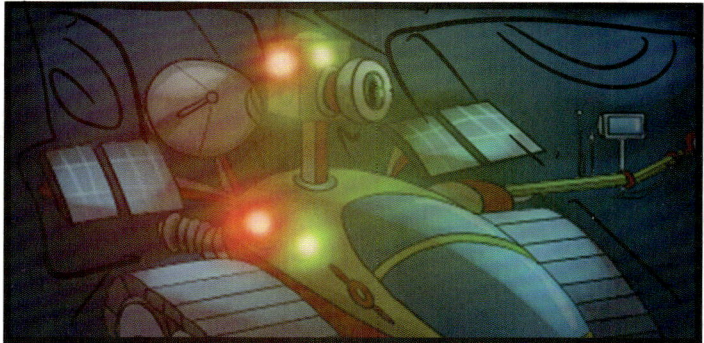

OUTSIDE THE AIRPORT:
I'VE BEEN WAITING FOR TWO HOURS ALREADY...
BUT I STILL HAVEN'T SEEN THE MAN I WAS HIRED TO KIDNAP.
I DON'T UNDERSTAND WHAT WENT WRONG.
THIS WAS SUPPOSED TO BE A SIMPLE MAFIA OPERATION. INVITE THE TARGET INTO MY CAR, LOCK THE DOORS, AND DRIVE OFF. I DON'T UNDERSTAND WHAT'S GOING ON...
ONE MINUTE. IS THAT HIM?
THIS MAN HAS A BEARD... CAN IT BE A DISGUISE?
HE ALSO HAS CHILDREN WITH HIM. STRANGE.

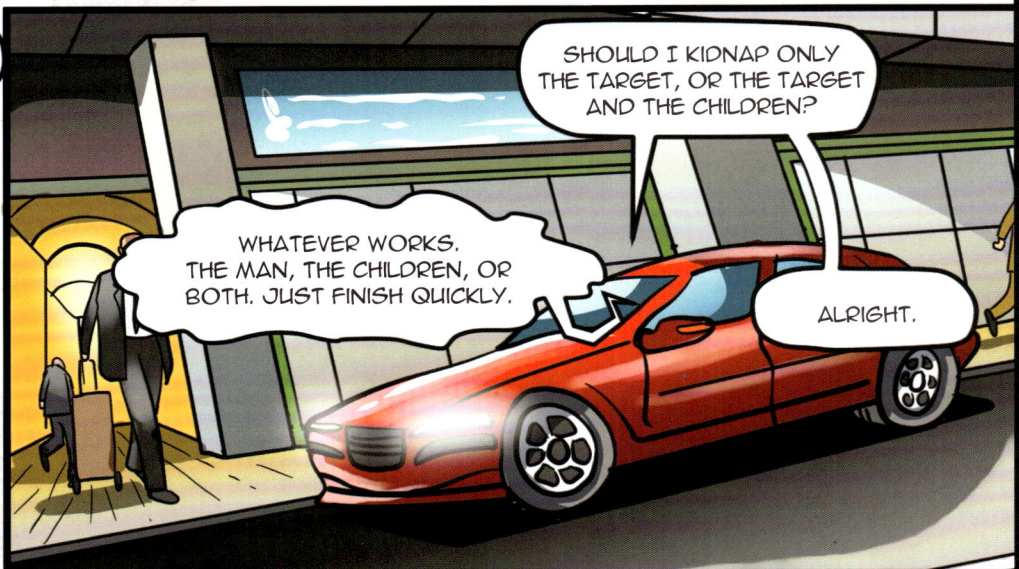

ABBA, WE'RE RIGHT HERE!

HEY! WHERE ARE YOU GOING, MISTER? OUR FATHER'S COMING TOO!

WHAT'S GOING ON? WHERE ARE YOU TAKING US?

WHAT'S HAPPENING?!

HE'S DRIVING LIKE A MANIAC – AND WE'RE HERE ALONE!

ROBI'S HERE TOO. ROBI'S HERE WITH YOU TOO.

WHAT DID YOU JUST SEE THROUGH YOUR BINOCULARS? WHERE DO YOU THINK WE ARE?

I DON'T NEED MY BINOCULARS TO KNOW THAT WE'RE IN THE JUNGLE.

YOU DIDN'T REALLY THINK I COULD BRING YOU BACK TO THE AIRPORT, EH? THE POLICE WOULD BE WAITING THERE TO CATCH ME.

THE JUNGLE?

ROBI DOESN'T LIKE THE JUNGLE. WHAT'S A JUNGLE?

THIS ISN'T A JUNGLE, BOYS. IT'S A SMALL FOREST.

THERE ARE NO POLICE HERE, ONLY ANIMALS.

ANIMALS?

I HOPE WE DON'T SEE ANY ELEPHANTS, SNAKES, OR EVEN FLIES. I HEARD SOME INSECTS AROUND HERE CARRY DANGEROUS DISEASES.

ZZZZZZ...

THE GANG MEMBERS MEET AT A NEARBY LIGHTHOUSE.

I DON'T UNDERSTAND WHY WE HAD TO COME ALL THE WAY OUT HERE.

WE NEEDED A MORE SECRET LOCATION TO FINALIZE OUR PLANS.

I HATE THAT IT'S SO DARK HERE.

WE COULDN'T RISK HAVING PEOPLE FIND OUT ABOUT OUR PLANS...

FINE. BUT LET'S FINISH QUICKLY.

PATIENCE. WE'LL LEAVE WHEN EVERYTHING IS COMPLETELY READY.

LET'S JUST GET OUT OF THIS SPOOKY PLACE.

I THINK WE CAN DRINK TO THE SUCCESS OF OUR MISSION ALREADY.

TOO BAD MR. BEN DAVID ISN'T HERE WITH US NOW.

HE'S AT THE AIRPORT, ACCORDING TO PLAN.

HISSSS.

WE NEED A MIRACLE TO GET OUT OF THIS JUNGLE ALIVE.

MAYBE THIS BRANCH CAN HELP US.

HERE'S ANOTHER BRANCH FOR ME.

WHOOSH... WHOOSH...

DO YOU HEAR THAT, ELI?

HEAR WHAT? A LION? A PACK OF HYENAS? A WOLF?

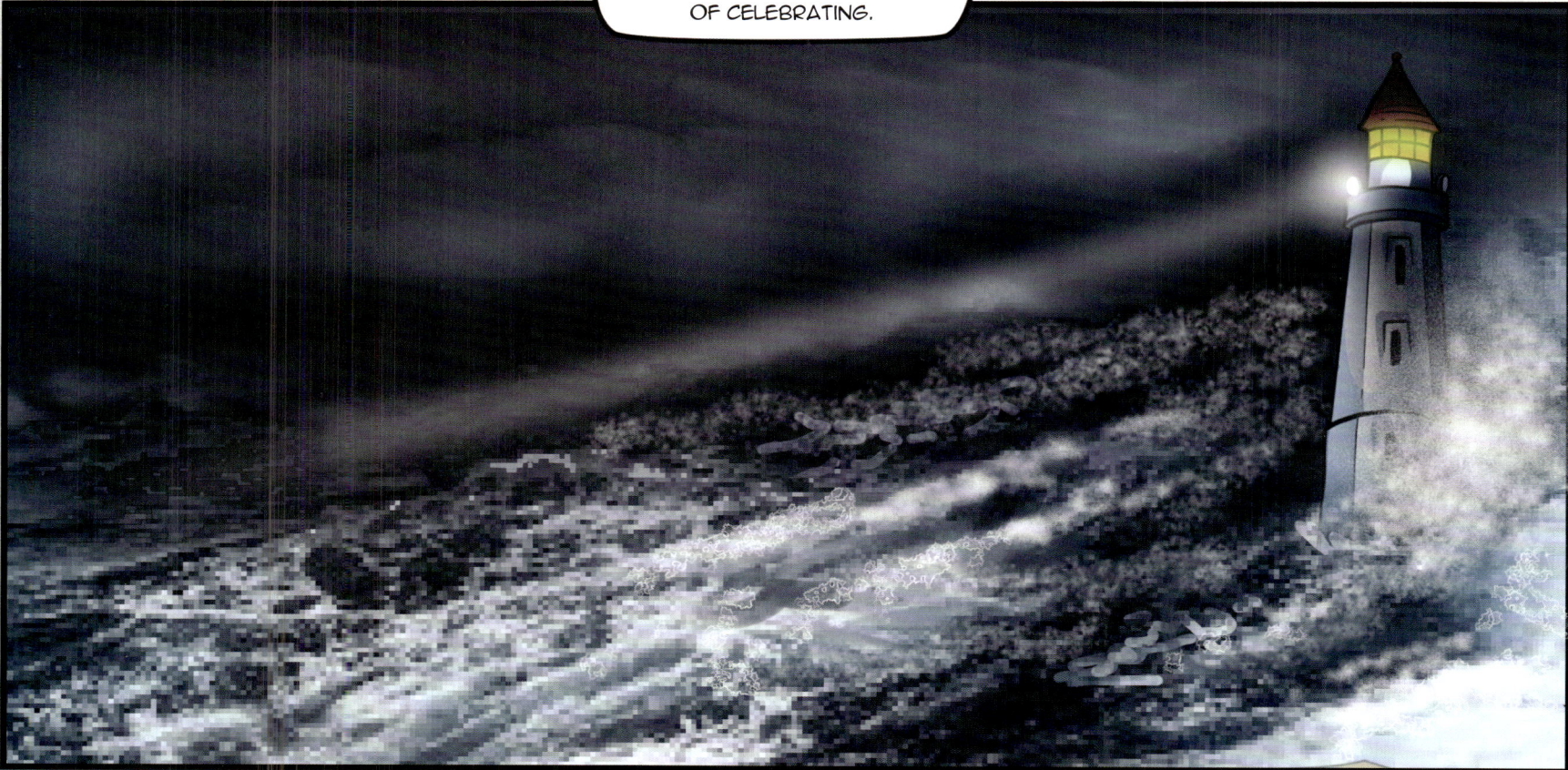

ER... THERE'S A FLOOD GOING ON...

IT'S ONLY A BIT OF RAIN. STOP EXAGGERATING.

THIS IS MORE THAN A BIT! WE NEED TO GET OUT OF HERE!

THE LIGHT HOUSE IS SHAKING!

HELP! HELP!

LET'S GET OUT QUICKLY!

WE'RE IN DEEP TROUBLE...

WE WON'T BE ABLE TO USE THIS BOAT OUT IN THE OCEAN.

WE DON'T EXACTLY HAVE A CHOICE.

I WISH THERE WAS SOMEPLACE FOR US TO DOCK.

HEY! WE CAN DOCK OVER THERE.

RIGHT! LEFT! RIGHT! LEFT! FORWARD!

I'M SCARED!

STORMY SEA! STORMY SEA!

OUR BOAT'S ABOUT TO CAPSIZE! HASHEM, PLEASE SAVE US!

SHIR HAMAALOS...

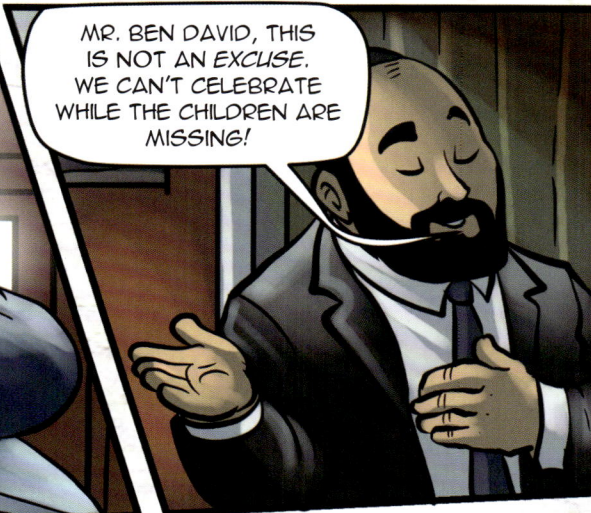

MEANWHILE...
SOMEONE'S CALLING.
WE NEED TO ANSWER THE PHONE.
RRRING!
CAREFUL! THERE'S A BIG WAVE COMING!
WAIT! WATCH OUT!
SPLASH!
GOOD THING ONLY THE PHONE FELL INTO THE WATER AND NOT US!
C'MON, I NEED YOUR HELP.
CAREFUL!

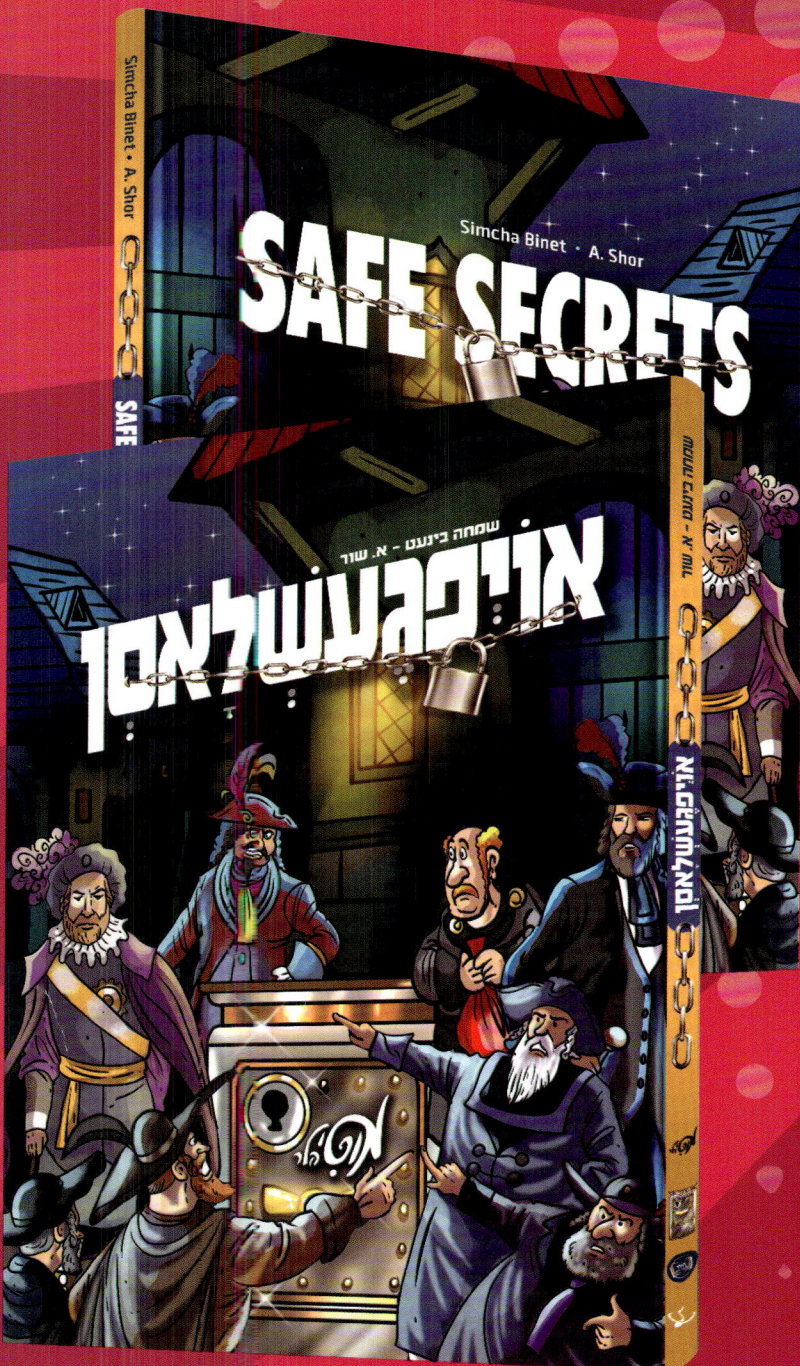

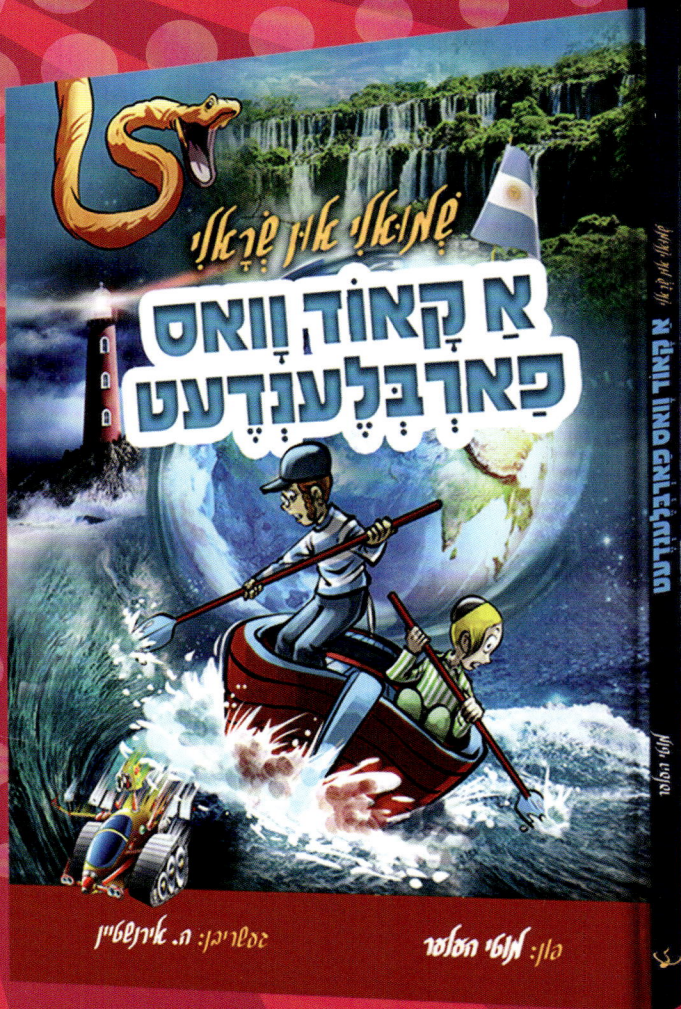

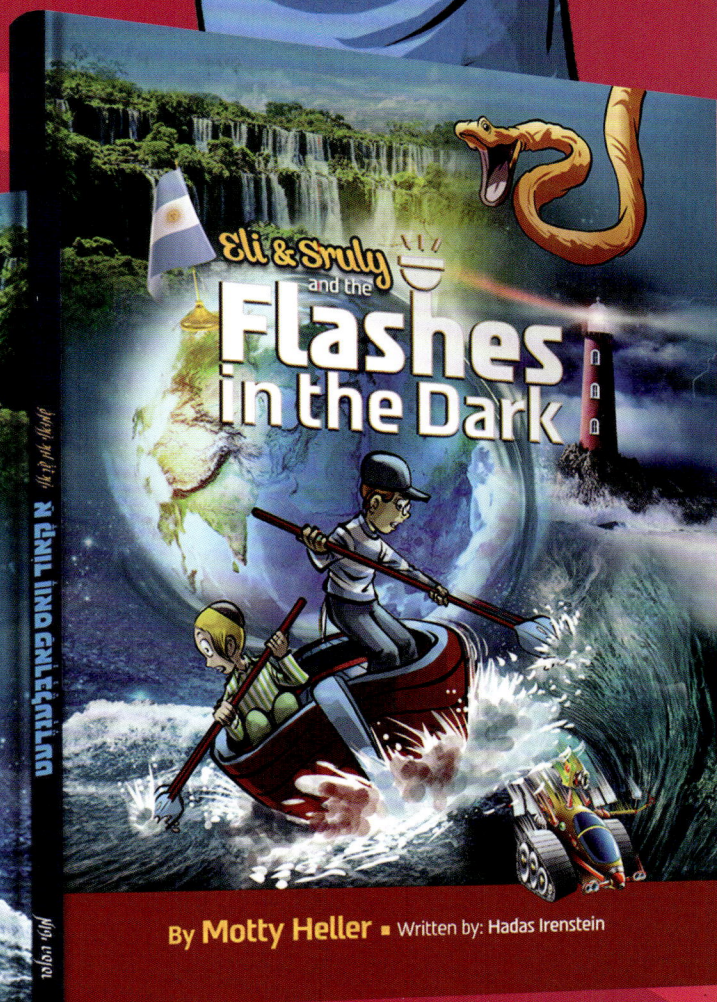

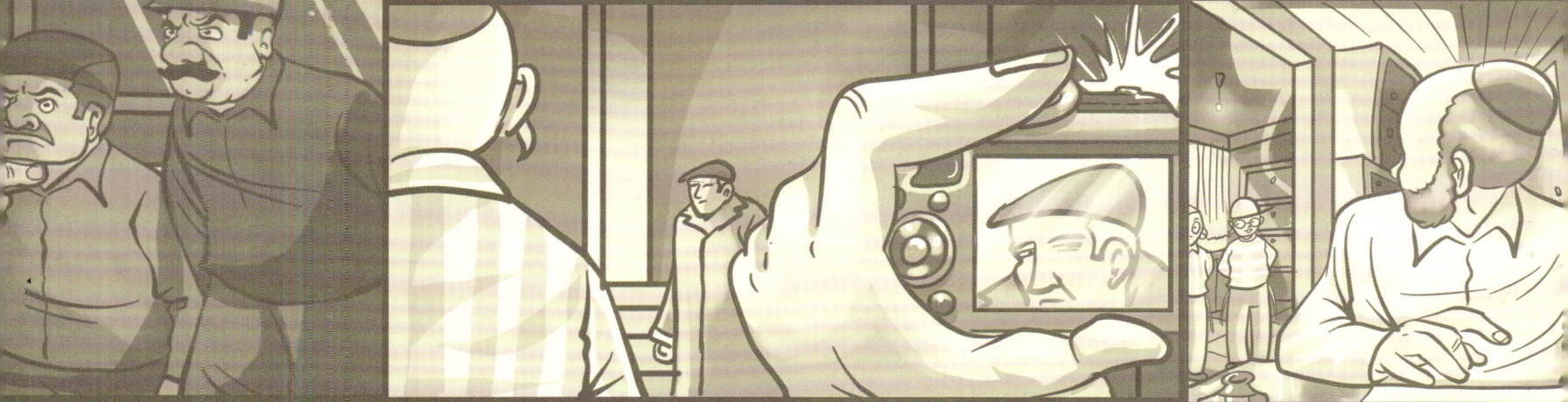